Radiance

Radiance

Poems by Barbara Crooker

Barbara Crooker (signature)

Word Press

*For Liz,
wishing you love
+ light in your life,
best,
Barbara
Catherines e. friend* (handwritten inscription)

© 2005 by Barbara Crooker

Published by Word Press
P.O. Box 541106
Cincinnati, OH 45254-1106

Typeset in Iowan Old Style by WordTech Communications
LLC, Cincinnati, OH

ISBN: 1932339914
LCCN: 2004116495

Poetry Editor: Kevin Walzer
Business Editor: Lori Jareo

Visit us on the web at www.word-press.com

Cover: Thomas Worthington Whittredge, *Kaaterskill Falls,* c.
1865, Oil on canvas, 19.5 x 15.5 inches, Private Collection.

Acknowledgments

America: "Impressionism"

Borderlands: "Some October"

Buckle &: "In Provence," "Away in Virginia, I See a Mustard Field"

Christianity and Literature: "Poem Ending with a Line by Rumi"

The Christian Century: "Sometimes, I Am Startled Out of Myself,"

The Christian Science Monitor: "Promise"

Cider Press Review: "Happiness"

Comstock Poetry Review: "The Grid"

Controlled Burn: "White Lilacs"

Cream City Review: "Corny"

Drunken Boat: "Grammar Lesson," "Van Gogh's Crows"

Earth's Daughters: "Red,"

International Review of Poetry: "All There Is to Say"

Karamu: "The Comet and the Opossum," "Nearing Menopause, I Run Into Elvis at Shoprite,"

The MacGuffin: "In Paris"

The Merton Seasonal: "Poem Ending with a Line by Rumi"

Midnight Mind: "Stand Up, Stand Up"

New Millennium Writing: "Nocturne in Blue"

New Zoo Poetry Review: "Twenty-five Years of Rejection Slips,"

One Trick Pony: "Against Nostalgia"

Parting Gifts: "October Lights the Woods"

Passager: "Poem for My Birthday"

The Pittsburgh Post-Gazette: "This Time of Year"

Poet Lore: "The Unfinished Work in Blue and Gold"

Poetry International: "The Gyre," "The Hour of Peonies"

Potomac Review: "A Congregation of Grackles," "The Woman Who Called Hawks from the Sky"

Rattle: "The Fifties"

Rhino: "The Deconstruction of Snow"

Smartish Pace: "Books Reviewed in *The New York Times*"

Solo: "Deep"

Two Rivers Review: "Why Monday Mornings Do Not Resemble the Shozui Temple," "Writers' Colony"

The Valparaiso Poetry Review: "All There Is to Say"

West Branch: " A Woman Is Pegging Wash on the Line," "Junior High, Home Economics," "Possibly," "Vegetable Love," "Star of Wonder"

Windhover: "Praise Song"

Yarrow: "Bricks," "In the Middle," "Quiscalus Quiscula"

"Possibly," "Red," "Vegetable Love," "A Woman Is Pegging Wash," "In the Middle," and "Quiscalus Quiscula" appeared in the chapbook *In the Late Summer Garden,* H & H Press, 1998. "Nocturne in Blue," "In Paris," "Sunflowers," and "Van Gogh's Crows" appeared in the folio collection *Paris,* sometimes y publications, 2002. "Nocturne in Blue" and "Nearing Menopause" appeared in *Greatest Hits,* Pudding House Publications, 2003. "Impressionism," "White Lilacs," "The Gyre," "Nocturne in Blue," "The Hour of Peonies," "In Paris," "In Provence," "Van Gogh's Crows," "Sunflowers," "The Unfinished Work in Blue and Gold," "Iris, 1889," "Away in Virginia, I See a Mustard Field and Think of You," "The Irrational Numbers of Longing," "Nature Morte au Plate et Pommes," "In Aix-en-Provence," and "All There Is to Say" appeared in *Impressionism,* Grayson Books, 2004.

"In the Middle" also appeared in the anthologies *Bless the Day* (Kodansha America) and *Proposing on the Brooklyn Bridge: Poems About Marriage* (Grayson Books). "Nearing Menopause" also appeared in the anthology *Grow Old Along With Me* (Papier Mache), in the audiotape version which was a 1997 Grammy Awards finalist, and in *Boomer Girls* (University of Iowa Press). "Red," and "A Woman Is Pegging Wash on the Line" also appeared in *The Cuirt Poetry Journal* (Ireland). "Nocturne in Blue" also appeared in *Le Train Blue* (France). "Vegetable Love" appeared in the anthology *Take Two, They're Small* (Outrider Press). "Van Gogh's Crows" appeared in the anthology *Beat the Blackened Wing*. "Nearing Menopause" appeared in *Hymns to the Outrageous* (Pudding House Press). "In the Middle" appeared in *Good Poems for Bad Times,* edited by Garrison Keillor (Viking Penguin). "Twenty-five Years of Rejection Slips" appeared in *Regrets Only* (Little Pear Press). "Promise" and "Sometimes I Am Startled Out of Myself" appeared in *Comfort Prayers* (Andrews McMeel.) "Praise Song" and "Promise" appeared in *Poetry Calendar* (Source Books).

"All That Is Glorious Around Us" won the W.B. Yeats Society of New York Award for 2004, judged by Grace Schulman. "Impressionism" was a finalist for the Foley Award. "Poem Ending with a Line by Rumi" won the Thomas Merton Poetry of the Sacred Prize, judged by Stanley Kunitz. "White Lilacs" won the "April Is the Cruelest Month" competition, sponsored by Poets & Writers. "Breath," "Possibly," "Leaving the White In," and "A Woman Is Pegging Wash on the Line" were Pushcart nominees. "The Grid" won honorable mention in *The Comstock Review* poetry contest. "Some October" won second place, Readers' Choice Awards, from *Orbis.* "The Comet and the Opossum" won honorable mention in the *Karamu* Poetry Contest. "Nocturne in Blue" won first place in the Y2K Competition from *New Millennium Writings.* "Nearing Menopause, I Run Into Elvis at Shoprite," "Away in Virginia, I See a Mustard Field and Think of You," and "In the Middle" were read on *The Writer's Almanac* by Garrison Keillor. "Nocturne in Blue" was read twice on the Australian Broadcasting Company's radio show, *Poetica.*

Many thanks to the Pennsylvania Council on the Arts for grants, to the Virginia Center for the Creative Arts for the time and space in which to work, and to Barbara Reisner, Kathy

Moser, Geri Rosenzweig, and Diane Lockward for their good
eyes and ears.

encore, for Richard

You sit in the midst of immense love, not alone
Marilyn Krysl

Contents

I

All That Is Glorious Around Us
(title of an exhibit on The Hudson River School)

is not, for me, these grand vistas, sublime peaks, mist-filled
overlooks, towering clouds, but doing errands on a day
of driving rain, staying dry inside the silver skin of the car,
160,000 miles, still running just fine. Or later,
sitting in a café warmed by the steam
from white chicken chili, two cups of dark coffee,
watching the red and gold leaves race down the street,
confetti from autumn's bright parade. And I think
of how my mother struggles to breathe, how few good days
she has now, how we never think about the glories
of breath, oxygen cascading down our throats to the lungs,
simple as the journey of water over rock. *It is the nature
of stone / to be satisfied /* writes Mary Oliver, *It is the nature
of water / to want to be somewhere else,* rushing down
a rocky tor or high escarpment, the panoramic landscape
boundless behind it. But everything glorious is around
us already: black and blue graffiti shining in the rain's
bright glaze, the small rainbows of oil on the pavement,
where the last car to park has left its mark on the glistening
street, this radiant world.

Impressionism

I'm sitting here doing nothing, soaking up
the late fall sunlight as if my life depended on it,
which, maybe it does, the end of a difficult year,
horror after horror on the news, my mother's life
decreasing breath by suffering breath. Too much death
for anyone to take in, and what comes next? The borders
of the world constrict, tighten. France now seems
like an impossible dream, as far away as the stars—
Over there, Renoir's villagers are still dazzled and dappled
by the sun at the *Moulin de la Galette*, and petit déjeuner
in a garden of irises or an aperatif of *vin rouge* and a bowl
of olives under dusty plane trees are *encore paradis*.
Somewhere in Normandy, apple trees bloom, pink and white.
In Provence, hills of ochre are balanced by a sky
of saturated blue. Monet's waterlilies open
and close in the pond at Giverny. I want to step out
of my life into a painting, perhaps Van Gogh's *Café
de la Nuit*. There I'll sit with my glass of absinthe
and a Gaulois bleu, until sweet forgetfulness takes me,
and the troubles of this world dissolve into daubs
of paint, a blizzard of color and light.

The Irrational Numbers of Longing, The Infinite Mathematics of Desire

This day could be reduced to three elements:
green grass, blue hills, yellow fields of mustard,
solid in its planes as any late Cézanne. It makes me think
of the curves your hips and back make when you are sleeping,
the way my fingers travel the back road of your spine,
the landscape of our bodies under the quilt.

I want to relearn the language of plane geometry,
the relationship of curves in space, the friction
between positive and negative numbers, improper
fractions, your lovely smooth surface, the angle
of intersection, where we come together in the dark.

Some October

Some October, when the leaves turn gold, ask
me if I've done enough to deserve this life
I've been given. A pile of sorrows, yes, but joy
enough to unbalance the equation.

When the sky turns blue as the robes of heaven,
ask me if I've made a difference.
The road winds through the copper-colored woods;
no one sees around the bend.

Today, the wind poured out of Canada,
a river in flood, bringing down the brilliant leaves,
broken sticks and twigs, deserted nests.
Go where the current takes you.

Some twilight, when the clouds stream in from the west
like the breath of God, ask me again.

Autism Poem: The Grid

A black and yellow spider hangs motionless in its web,
and my son, who is eleven and doesn't talk, sits
on a patch of grass by the perennial border, watching.
What does he see in his world, where geometry
is more beautiful than a human face?
Given chalk, he draws shapes on the driveway:
pentagons, hexagons, rectangles, squares.
The spider's web is a grid,
transecting the garden in equal parts.

Sometimes he stares through the mesh on a screen.
He loves things that are perforated:
toilet paper, graham crackers, coupons
in magazines, loves the order of the tiny holes,
the way the boundaries are defined. And real life
is messy and vague. He shrinks back to a stare,
switches off his hearing. And my heart,
not cleanly cut like a valentine, but irregular
and many-chambered, expands and contracts,
contracts and expands.

II

The Comet and the Opossum

The opossum that used to live in the thorny tangle
of wild roses is dead this winter; I found his body
as the snow melted, the same March that the Comet Hyakutake
passed us by. I've been out these clear nights looking
at its smudgy brightness as it travels across
the constellations, Virgo to Boötes to the Big Dipper
and the little one. Now it's just west of Cassiopeia,
in Perseus. I try to imagine 20,000 years ago, the last
time it came by, when we were living in skins and caves,
seeing it trail its luminous tail across the known patterns,
the atavistic shiver. When I take my nightly walk, I fix
on the comet around every bend in the road. Each night, it
has moved one notch west. Every day when I walk the dog,
the opossum's fur has eroded a little more, bone showing
through, the teeth set in a primitive snarl. He came
to the back door one winter, but only one, and ate the scraps
of meat and fat set out for the birds. One night, he curled
up in the wheelbarrow, hissed when we came too close.
Now, he diminishes daily, as insects and weather
do their work, until only a few clumps of fur remain,
and meadow rue and lady's bedstraw begin to cover the bones.
Last night, looking up at the inky blackness, I felt myself
shrink, smaller than the smallest bones in the opossum's tail,
and then I found the comet one last time. It seemed to be fixed
in the firmament, a nebulous white light in the western sky,
but was, like this transient world, rapidly drifting away.

The Deconstruction of Snow

For snow itself is an absence—
it blots out the blue sky
stippled with clouds,
the demarcation of heaven and earth,
sidewalk and street, garden and lawn.

Just try to catch
it with sketchpad, camera,
notebook—it drifts blamelessly
through our fingers.

Attempt to pin it down on black velvet
like a Great Spangled Fritillary,
Mourning Cloak, or some other
Lepidoptera. Hah. Not in *this*
postmodern universe. Realism,
Naturalism, those quaint notions
we still carry, like metal lunchboxes
with Roy Rogers or Rin Tin Tin.

And all those old fairy tales—
Snow White, with her lips
red as blood, hair like night,
skin white as the great etc.,
why, they're narratives—
linear, how bizarre.

Meanwhile, high above us,
in the great kitchen of the clouds,
the Chief Pastry Chef
is sifting, sifting.
(There's that darned allusion
slipping in again,

silent as the fall of flake
on flake.)

And that same old self-referential snow,
noun and verb at the same time,
keeps on falling
in straight lines,
telling its story
to anyone
who will listen.

But no matter.
The text is everything.
The only thing.
The rest is
diamond-dazzled
glitter-feathered
hexagonal-crystalled
silence.

Star of Wonder, Star of Light

It's Christmas, the year before the accident, when the earth
still seemed fixed. My husband and children are hanging
lights on the big pine tree, the one that Becky
brought home as a seedling in first grade wrapped in a damp
paper towel. I am cooking dinner while they struggle
with the wires that somehow knot themselves up in the box.
Shadows gather behind the hills. The tree turns dark green,
then black. The tangled string unravels, and they pass it
around, loop over loop, while I watch from the steamy window:
husband, son, and daughter in a circle around the tree,
their arms full of stars.

Nocturne in Blue

She asked me to bring her back a stone
from Paris, where even the dirt is historic,
but I wanted, instead, to find her the color
of *l'heure bleu*, the shimmer of twilight

with the street lamps coming on, the way they keep
the dark back for just a little while, the reflections
of headlamps and taillights, red and gold, on the Champs
d'Élysees wet with rain and a fog rising.

And there's the way the past becomes a stone,
how you carry it with you, lodged in your pocket.
The blue light deepens, evening's melancholy shawl,
the wide boulevard of the Seine, the way the stones

of the monuments become watery, ripple in the currents
and the wind. Everything seems eternal here,
to us from the West, who have no memory of dates
like 52 BC, 1066, the *fin de siècle*

as we barge on past the millennium,
history's crazy swirl, oil on pavement,
a promenade down *les Grands Boulevards*.
This is what I'd bring back: shadows of stones,

twilight longings, a handful of crushed lilacs
from the bar at the Closerie, some lavender de Provence,
Odilon Redon's chalky mauves, a jazz piano playing the blues,
Mood Indigo; just a condensation of blue,
distilled in a small glass bottle with a stopper,
as if it came from an expensive *parfumerie*,
musk of the centuries, the gathering dusk,
a hedge against night, the world that will end.

A Congregation of Grackles

It is the season of no return, winter not done
with us, spring yet to arrive. Scruffy lawns
turn a little greener; daylight preens, spreads
its feathers. Grackles fan their wings,
clatter and clack in the maple trees,
making a racket that passes for song.
Startled, they pour out of the woods,
a long black scarf unwinding
in the cold west wind.
Their raucous talk, a thousand fingernails
scratching on glass or a chalkboard,
shreds the air. Black cross stitches,
embroidering the blue bunting sky,
they are the X, the unknown quantity
in every equation. They mark the spot
where we cross the equinox,
the resurrection of the woods,
moving from darkness
into the light.

III

Sometimes, I Am Startled Out of Myself,

like this morning, when the wild geese came squawking,
flapping their rusty hinges, and something about their trek
across the sky made me think about my life, the places
of brokenness, the places of sorrow, the places where grief
has strung me out to dry. And then the geese come calling,
the leader falling back when tired, another taking her place.
Hope is borne on wings. Look at the trees. They turn to gold
for a brief while, then lose it all each November.
Through the cold months, they stand, take the worst
weather has to offer. And still, they put out shy green leaves
come April, come May. The geese glide over the cornfields,
land on the pond with its sedges and reeds.
You do not have to be wise. Even a goose knows how to find
shelter, where the corn still lies in the stubble and dried stalks.
All we do is pass through here, the best way we can.
They stitch up the sky, and it is whole again.

Possibly

When I left Pennsylvania, spring was still scuffing her feet,
scarf muffled around her neck, duffle coat buttoned up tight,
the ground still hard as a calculus textbook, grass infinite
shades of dun and tan, the scruffy pelt of something dead
by the road, trees and branches bare.
I was heavy as lead, the low grey sky, cold front moving in,
calendar flipping back to March. You and I sat in separate
rooms with our books, at odds and elbows; our busy
lives with their datebooks and daytimers filling in the blanks.
But I'm coming back now, sweet as bird song, right as rain,
new poems in my notebook that flutter from my wrists
like those first new leaves that suddenly appear on a warm day.
And now it is the hour of lemon light, forsythia wands
shooting sparks over the new grass, daffodils showering gold
in the wind. It is the season of possibility, when anything
might happen. Two stubborn people, dulled into habit,
stuck in the old sock of marriage, might just fall in love again,
watch the sun set behind the orchard, watch the sky turn lilac
and lavender, feel the stars click into their new stories,
soft air on their arms, soft breath in the mouth.
They might start to do the old dance, the spring dance,
the clothes are in the way dance, the return of blue scilla
skies dance; they might rub lilac blossoms all over their skin.

Promise

This day is an open road
stretching out before you.
Roll down the windows.
Step into your life, as if it were a fast car.
Even in industrial parks,
trees are covered with white blossoms,
festive as brides, and the air is soft
as a well-washed shirt on your arms.
The grass has turned implausibly green.
Tomorrow, the world will begin again,
another fresh start. The blue sky stretches,
shakes out its tent of light. Even dandelions glitter
in the lawn, a handful of golden change.

Stand Up, Stand Up

Driving through the Blue Ridge Mountains, Sunday morning,
early April, the bare woods like an eager congregation
waiting for the service to begin. I scan the radio,
and find The Hour of Beautiful Gospel & Spiritual Music
near Forks of the Buffalo, sponsored by the fine folks
of the Carl B. Hutchinson Funeral Home, who stand ready
to be with you in your hour of need. They promise
an electric organ, an air-conditioned chapel, and ample
parking. *I cried, my Lord, for my way is dark,*
I need your light down in my heart. I hear songs by
The Joyful Noise, the Kingdom-Aires, Heaven Bound,
and First Love Revival, while road signs advertising
Seed Clothes and Red Angus Bulls 4 Sale speed by.
My burdens begin to lift, my heart feels light
as a white winged dove. *Nothing can erase God's grace,*
the past would not let go. It burned like an ember,
when I did remember . . . .
Dogwoods sing glad hosannas, out in full bloom
even before the leaves. The station fades; in Winchester,
Virginia, I find Southern Light, The Power of Positive Radio.
When He said, "It is finished," it was just the beginning for me.
There's a Spring Bible sale on at the Center Point Bookstore,
and this hour is sponsored by Ron Martin Appliance,
"We're not perfect, but we sure do try hard."
I believe in miracles; I'm a miracle myself.
On either side of the Interstate (*I want to find, find the road*
that leads to Heaven's door), newly green fields, brown & white
cows, the long stretch of the Blue Ridge, and solid yellow fields
of mustard *bright shining as the sun.* And all along the highway,
more and more redbuds, as if God's hand had scribbled in fuchsia
along the brown bark, a loud shout of gladness, joy in my rocky,
rocky heart.

Away In Virginia, I See a Mustard Field and Think of You

because the blue hills are like the shoulders and slopes
of your back as you sleep. Often, I slip a hand under
your body to anchor myself to this earth. The yellow
mustard rises from a waving sea of green.

I think of us driving narrow roads in France, under
a tunnel of sycamores, my hair blowing in the hot wind,
opera washing out of the radio, loud. We are feeding
each other cherries from a white paper sack.

And then we return to everyday life, where we fall
into bed exhausted, fall asleep while still reading,
forget the solid planes of the body in the country
of dreams. I miss your underwear, soft from a thousand
washings, the socks you still wear from a store
out of business thirty years. I love to smell your sweat
after mowing grass or hauling wood; I miss the weight
on your side of the bed.

White Lilacs
after a painting by Edouard Manet

In the last year of his life, wretchedly shortened through illness,
Manet painted several of these vases of simple flowers.
Sister Wendy, The Book of Meditations

When the world
was reduced to a black flag
of pain, what else could he do
but paint flowers, white
lilacs in a crystal vase,
prismatic in the May sunlight,
their heavy perfume
filling the room?

And what can I do
when my autistic son
shuts down, talks nonsense,
flicks and stims?
I want to go out
and swim in this river
of drenching scent,
so thick you could lick it
from the air. I'd like to shrink
to the size of a raindrop,
make my home on this branch
of white clusters, let the ether
of their odor anesthetize the evening,
a field of blank white snow.

The Gyre

Last night, the owl woke me;
I heard him ask the moon
in his rising tremolo, *who who who?*
Unable to sleep, I thought of Monet
at eighty, painting waterlilies, pond, and sky
over 250 times. He wrote, "These landscapes of water
and reflections have become an obsession for me."

And my compulsive son asks questions without answers
ad infinitum in an endless loop: "What time is 12 o'clock
midnight? When is it Saturday? Where is Hurricane
Floyd? Will you marry me all the time?"
Over and over, he pinches, face, arms, and chest.

Monet said, "Each day, I discover things I didn't see
before," but I lie here wondering how I can get through
another day of this. I ask the owl *why why why?*
but he doesn't reply, and the full moon,
that great blank disk in the sky, keeps on shining.

Iris, 1889
Vincent Van Gogh

Out of the stony ground of his tortured life, these iris
rise, writhe, charmed like snakes by the song of the sun.
The wild blue heart of longing moves up, up,
from papery rhizomes, common dirt. Out of nothing,
armfuls of sky. They burn, flames in a hearth, as they dance
above the pale green swords of their leaves. It's all
or nothing, this loud shout, this wild abundance, a few short
weeks in May. On the canvas, they sing forever. The suffering
world recedes in the background. They lean to the left, pushed
by the wind, but not one stalk is bent or broken. Oh, the fierce
burning joys of this life; all the things of the world, about to vanish.

The Hour of Peonies

The Buddha says, "Breathing in, I know I am here in my body.
Breathing out, I smile to my body," and here I am, mid-span,
a full-figured woman who could have posed for Renoir.
When I die, I want you to plant peonies for me, so each May,
my body will resurrect itself in these opulent blooms, one
of *les Baigneuses*, sunlight stippling their luminous breasts,
rosy nipples, full bellies, an amplitude of flesh, *luxe, calme
et volupté*. And so are these flowers, an exuberance
of cream, pink, raspberry, not a shrinking violet
among them. They splurge, they don't hold back,
they spend it all. At the end, confined to a wheelchair,
paintbrushes strapped to his arthritic hands,
Renoir said, "the limpidity of the flesh, one wants to caress it."
Even after the petals have fallen, the lawn is full of snow,
the last act in Swan Lake where the corps de ballet,
in their feathered tutus,
kneel and kiss the ground, cover it in light.

Quiscalus Quiscula

On the lawn, the grackles spread their nightdark fans,
cluck softly to themselves. They are telling me,
"Get back to work." They are telling me time
is rushing like a river, restless. They are saying
tomorrow may be too late. Their yellow eyes
glint like the clasp of a satin purse.
Consider then, these birds of the air.
Their heads shine in the sun,
an anti-iridescence. Their bodies are glazed
in bronze. They cluck their tongues in sorrow
for the world gone wrong, or what we've failed to do.
Is the purpose for their darkness to fly against
the dogwoods, remind us that night is always
bearing down? Time beats its blueblack wings,
elusive, hopping from branch to branch
in the sweet cerise of the flowering crab.
These grackles are angels of the Lord,
and we are just fooled by their robes of soot.
They speak in tongues; whole glossolalia rolls
out of their beaks. Their song is unmusical, industrial,
like a wrench on metal. They rise in a dark river,
fly past the redbuds next to the cherries, a small stream
of violets underneath, it's over-the-top, the Fauvism
of spring. Maybe the blackbird's song is an inexplicable
mystery, or as plain as black and blue:
Love whatever you can.

IV

Twenty-five Years of Rejection Slips,

and what does it matter? How many trees have been pulped
for this constant susurrus: sending, resending,
        shuffling, sorting?
Even the name *submission* suggests a certain deference,
servility, prostration: lying down in front of the mailbox,
and letting the great steamroller of indifference flatten
me into the ground. You could read the morning newspaper
through my bones. Maybe here is the lesson: Look
at the wind, how it turns the pages of the leaves, riffles
through chapter after chapter, whispers countless stories
that no one bothers to write down. Look at the stanzas
of light in the locust leaves as they bob and weave
in the hot July wind, their effortless green repetition
and refrain. Why not give it up now? The phone isn't going
to ring; the mailbox is full of circulars and bills. So maybe
I'll read to the cardinals and wrens, sink back in the hammock,
listen to the hot buzz of the cicadas' applause.
Look, clouds are writing their manuscripts on the big blue book
of the sky. They don't fear the wind's erasure, or night's
emphatic black rejection. Tomorrow, a clean sheet comes up
in the roller, and we'll start all over again.

Sunflowers

This time of year, the hot sun spiralling down on the farmlands,
makes me think about Van Gogh's wheat fields, the unrelenting
light, sky scratched with crows, their dark raucous chatter—
and I think about our short lives, chaff in the wind,
momentary in the darkening sky. I think about
his cypresses, their black flames, his bruise-blue
irises that wince against the yellow wall, the vase
of sunflowers, those molten golds, the fierceness
of their burning. Even the blues, Vincent's blues,
the cobalt intensity behind the yellow house,
the thunderclouded sky, should cool us down, but don't.
Instead, they boil at low flame.
He said in a letter to his brother, "I am in it with all
of my heart," and I am in it, too, this life, with its longing
and sorrows. When we're gone, what will be left of our small
songs and minor joys? Still, when I drive by a wheat field
turning ochre and amber, every awn and arista shouting sun!
sun! sun! something in me rises, makes me look
for a scrap of paper, a pencil nub,
even as the hot wind lifts,
blows the dust we are, carries it away—

In Provence

Light of freshly pressed olive oil
spills through the plane trees
under whose deep shade-stippled branches
we sit, in a small *café*, glass of *vin rouge*,
clay bowl of olives. Van Gogh
might have painted this, light that could be
bottled, corked, so you could dip in a crust of bread
on a winter night when the *mistral* roars
down the *vallée du Rhône* like a deranged freight
train. Vincent wrote, "There is no blue without yellow,"
and you think of his house in Arles and the boiling sky;
the reapers sleeping in the wheat stacks, the azure field
of noon rising behind them; "La Nuit Étoilée," fiery
pinwheels floating in slashes of cobalt and cerulean,
the reflected lights casting their nets of gold
on the blueblack Rhône. . . .

Just as you and I walk along its banks tonight,
man and woman, light and reflection, point and counterpoint.
And if one of us goes on the last journey
into the long dark? There is no gold without blue, no yin
without yang, no me without you.

In Paris

A rectangle of light spills in the high window
over the porcelain tub in our small *hôtel*,
and a blackbird, a *merle*, is singing his strange *chanson*,
r's swallowed in the back of his throat, those palate-
ringing u's: *dur, truffes, du fluide, tu penses.*
At the rue de Varenne, Rodin's Thinker is still stuck
in the rose garden, his bronze thoughts lost
in translation. Across the lawn, in a smaller version,
he broods above *les Portes d'Enfer*:
Abandon hope, all ye who enter.
Underneath, eternity's lovers twine
about each other, the embrace of the damned,
yearn and long but never touch, all that unattainable
flesh. The twisting lovers try to hold on even
as they are torn away or melt backwards
into the liquid bronze night, condemned to writhe
in tortured high relief. But we are here, in our
middle-aged imperfect bodies, walking hand in hand
under an *allée* of plane trees in the dazzled light,
and my desire for you, even after all these years,
is a *marc*, an *eau-de-vie*, hot and heady
in the blood. High above us, chimney swifts,
les martinets, take up their nightly chorus, shrieking
as they swoop and dive for insects in the long dusk.
Praise the small cage of the elevator
that carries us to our *chambre*. Praise my four-
chambered heart, still beating; praise your gall
bladder, unremoved. O Paris, city of *café noir*
and *vin rouge*, where even the subway signs
are works of art, city of rapturous light,
ghosts of Hemingway and Stein at the Closerie,
Simone and Jean-Paul at the Café de Flor,
you and I, our little story nearly over,

singing loudly as we can, in our tone deaf voices,
against the coming rain and the following dark.

In Aix-en-Provence

Rectangles of light fall on Mount Sainte-Victoire,
as the colors shift, and evening's violet cashmere
softens the landscape. I'd like to edit out
the industrial world, keep only the ochre hills, the dark
umbrella pines, the cold blues of the mountain and sky.
Give me life without newspapers, e-mail, and faxes,
TV, DVD, video, radio; let me sit in the sun like a cat
while patches of shadow move over my arms
as the day wears on. Where breakfast is a flaky
roll that shatters when I bite it, that sings like the sun
in my mouth. Where lunch is a ripe pear, slab
of melting cheese, baton of bread, all crust;
and dinner, with its dark wine, white china, heavy silver,
waits like an orchestra tuning up in the wings. And the mountain
turns lilac, gold, rose; colors the air around it, falls on my hair,
my *crêpe de Chine* dress, and, for a while, erases time's tiny lines,
restores the smooth planes of my face, puts me back
in my younger skin. On the last day of my life, I'd like
to be working, like Cézanne, even if it means being pulled home
in a laundry cart and dying of pneumonia. I want to be out there,
singing, as the rain comes down, solid blocks of purple, blue.

Red,

red the cherries turn,
burning in the dark green sky,
a thousand suns, almost as red
as the true sun that's going down
right now behind the mock orange
and weigela, so hot you'd think
it would sizzle, hiss
as its light's put out
for the night.

At the heart of each cherry
there's a pit, a stone,
an architecture of bone,
the flesh ripening
so fast, so fast.
Robins steal the cherries one by one.
And who can blame them?
Such fierce burning.
This world, red in tooth
and claw, with so much loss
sometimes you wish
your heart could turn to stone.
But still, the flesh is sweet.

Now the sky darkens, and the cherries
cannot be seen. It is one of those soft
summer nights, after a day of bake oven heat,
the air playing with the hair on your neck,
the bare skin of your arms and legs.
In the grass, fireflies rise in their sultry dance,
little love notes that flicker, that burn.

Happiness
She loves West Tenth Street on an
ordinary summer morning.
(Michael Cunningham, The Hours)

And I love *this* ordinary summer afternoon,
sitting under my cherry tree full of overripe fruit,
too much for us to pick, an *abbonanza* of a tree,
I love this dark grey catbird singing its awkward song,
and the charcoal clouds promising rain they don't deliver.
I love the poem I've been trying to write for months,
but can't; I love the way it's going nowhere at all.
I love the dried grass that crackles when you walk on it,
leached of color, its own kind of fire.
Way off in the hedgerow, the musical olio of dozens of birds,
each singing its own song, each beating its own measure.
This is all there is: the red cherries, the green leaves,
sky like a pale silk dress, and the rise and fall
of the sweet breeze. Sometimes, just what you have
manages to be enough.

All There Is to Say
("Onions and Bottle," 1895, Cézanne)
"A painter can say all he wants to with fruit . . . ."
    Edouard Manet

or even vegetables, these crinkly-skinned onions
on a kitchen table, painted by Cézanne.
What did he want to tell us about their many layers,
their astringent flesh, pungent breath, thin skins?
Was it the way they could fill a plate, nestle in a table
cloth, look like they belonged there, eggs
in a nest? Or how they add depth to a stew
or a bouillabaisse without becoming the thing itself,
like the notes in a chord, or the blue wash that's part
of the undercoat, part of the shadow. Unlike other
still lifes, these onions are living: green shoots burst
out their tops, electric, wired, a green dance
of new growth. Green flames singing in the hearth.
Green fingers shooting for the sun. What else
could he want to say, except that every thing
on this small blue ball *is* alive, these papery globes,
the throat of the wine bottle, the billions of molecules
that make up my skin and yours, the air between our lips,
charged with energy, the cells that slough off
when they touch, when we love.

Vegetable Love

Feel a tomato, heft its weight in your palm,
think of buttocks, breasts, this plump pulp.
And carrots, mud clinging to the root,
gold mined from the earth's tight purse.
And asparagus, that push their heads up,
rise to meet the returning sun,
and zucchini, green torpedoes
lurking in the Sargasso depths
of their raspy stalks and scratchy leaves.
And peppers, thick walls of cool jade, a green hush.
Secret caves. Sanctuary.
And beets, the dark blood of the earth.
And all the lettuces: bibb, flame, oak leaf, butter-
crunch, black-seeded Simpson, chicory, cos.
Elizabethan ruffs, crisp verbiage.
And spinach, the dark green
of northern forests, savoyed, ruffled,
hidden folds and clefts.
And basil, sweet basil, nuzzled
by fumbling bees drunk on the sun.
And cucumbers, crisp, cool white ice
in the heart of August, month of fire.
And peas in their delicate slippers,
little green boats, a string of beads,
repeating, repeating.
And sunflowers, nodding at night,
then rising to shout hallelujah! at noon.

All over the garden, the whisper of leaves
passing secrets and gossip, making assignations.
All of the vegetables bask in the sun,
languorous as lizards.

Quick, before the frost puts out
its green light, praise these vegetables,
earth's voluptuaries,
praise what comes from the dirt.

Corny

I.

It was the summer without carbohydrates, call it Atkins,
the Zone, South Beach, call it what you will, but
we have said *no* to the grains, crusty bread,
tiny new potatoes; we've put pasta behind us, scorned
desserts: blueberry pie, plum duff, cherry crisp; not even
watermelon or Queen Anne cherries have crossed our lips.
We've stocked up on protein and forbidden fats, laced
everything with mayo, butter, and sour cream. But now
it's the season of sweet corn, nuggets of gold
swaddled in green, and we can't resist; we are helpless
to the call of tender kernels in checkerboard lines; our hunger
is enormous, our fingers itch to start. There's row after row
of typing waiting to be eaten; you can almost hear the bell ding
as you reach the end of the line. Butter-and-Sugar. Kandy Korn.
Ambrosia. Silver Queen. Sweet Symphony.

First, bring the water to full boil before you fill your arms
with ears. Get out a brick of pale butter, coarse salt. Husk
the outer leaves, peel the damp silk that wants to cling
to your hands, and plunge the yellow into that steam;
in five quick minutes, you'll be in corn heaven,
the sweetness ripening in your mouth, bits stuck in your teeth,
butter gleaming on your chin. O, my tasseled darling,
my sweetest heart, let's strip off all our leaves, lie down
in the stalks and shocks, and rub our beautiful yellow bodies
with salt, with light.

II

Sometimes, the days go on and on, boring as row after row
after row of green. Sometimes, you come around a bend
in the road and see it waving, and it's astonishing
as a jade green sea. Somewhere in Illinois, there's a camcorder
set in a field, and you can log on, sit back, and see the corn grow

from germination to emergence, dried-out pebbles to first green
shoots to sky-high stalks, ears growing plumper, tassels
springing out like everyone's fear of a bad hair day. You can
watch and watch, but you'll never actually see it happen;
despite our oceans of knowledge, what starts this ticking
is deep and dark as the dirt from which they sprang.

III
The day Jerry Garcia died, I ran into a friend
near the Ben & Jerry's at the Food Giant; row after row,
pints of Cherry Garcia glistened behind us.
Who could write about this, it's so corny? But it's true,
and the music we love loops on in our heads,
our own personal soundtrack. There's a kernel of truth
in every cliché, a term confused
by most freshman composition students,
who think it's synonymous with "clique,"
that sorting into hierarchical order
provided by American high schools.
And what's more American than corn-on-the-cob?
It ripens with the political conventions, is harvested
by Election Day. This field
yields to no one, not the Senator from Nebraska
nor the one from Kansas, not even in August.
If it's as high as an astronaut's eye, you know
it's a banner year, a bumper crop. Electioneering
is hungry work, all those hands waving like tassels
in a hot wind. Raise your placards: Iowa.
South Dakota. Oklahoma.
We're all casting our electoral votes now,
for corn. He who has ears, let him eat.

V

Books Reviewed in *The New York Times*, Sunday, June 9, 2002

When I Was a Girl, summers stretched forever;
Back Then, all those hours were my own, tall cool
tumblers waiting to be filled. I'd bike to the library,
Nancy Drews and Bobbsey Twins, their blue cardboard covers
faintly musty, stacked to the top of the wire basket that hung
over the fat front tire. *Deep in the Shade of Paradise*,
how could I know I was *Creating a Life* of words,
what I needed to bring me *Across Open Ground*,
where *The Sound of Trees* talking to each other
was conversation enough. Due dates were stamped
with a rubber wheel, inked from a black pad.
Some books, I couldn't return on time, paid the fine
with my own allowance. Years later, my first child
was born, then died, on her due date. Books were my salvation.
Nothing Remains the Same. Walk Through Darkness.

Autism Poem: Bricks

In the red brick Union Free School, upstate New York,
radiators hissed, and the smell of wet wool
and library paste hung in the air. Outside, it was snowing,
and the tall wooden windows were decorated with cut & fold
snowflakes and red paper hearts. Language was just
another tool, like pencils or chalk, for making something
to bring home and show. Spelling words were a game,
memorized for a gold star. Reading was grouped;
everyone knew that Bluebirds were the best.
Flash cards. Times tables. Drill, recite. Drill, recite.
The radiators' steam covered the windows. I glowed
in the yellow light, the teacher's praise. The stickers
and stars, the good report cards in their manila folders.
Years and years later, with a child who doesn't talk,
hyperlexic, echolalic—what did I know
of how to build a language brick by brick,
what kind of mortar could hold these words?

Grammar Lesson

(italicized line is from Jewel, *by Brett Lott)*

I come downstairs, late, an ordinary Saturday morning,
smell coffee and bagels, step over the old dog
dozing in the middle of the floor
in a wide rectangle of sun,
and maybe my hair is freshly washed,
and catches the light like a glossy wing,
or maybe you smell the vanilla
I've rubbed here and there,
but *that old language of our bodies is resurrected,*
and we move our fingers over familiar hills and valleys.
I breathe in your skin, the hair on the back of your neck,
you pull me down on your lap,
and leave the pile of bills
you were working on.
Yes, the television hums
its little babble, and our son
chatters and fiddles with Legos,
and yes, there's a long list
of errands to be run.
But we are conjugating familiar verbs,
decorating with adjectives,
building new sentences noun by noun.
We are remembering syntax, etymology,
why love began, the original sin.

Deep,

deep in the long green days of summer, the crescendos
of heat bugs rising in the noon sun, the hot air, thick
as a lake— So far into this marriage,
like a John Deere harvester in a field of corn,
a small green island planted right in the middle
of everything— Even the grass on the lawn breathes
longing, the complicated chemistry of light into sugar—
Sometimes, I feel the small hairs on my arm rise, ionic
as the air before a storm—And you are the clapper,
and I am the bell cast in bronze around you.
Before we slip into sleep's black waters,
we set the golden tones ringing,
ripples of moonlight falling on the bed sheets
and quilt, our bodies' music in the dark.

In the Middle

of a life that's as complicated as everyone else's,
struggling for balance, juggling time.
The mantle clock that was my grandfather's
has stopped at 9:20; we haven't had time
to get it repaired. The brass pendulum is still,
the chimes don't ring. One day I look out the window,
green summer, the next, the leaves have already fallen,
and a grey sky lowers the horizon. Our children almost grown,
our parents gone, it happened so fast. Each day, we must learn
again how to love, between morning's quick coffee
and evening's slow return. Steam from a pot of soup rises,
mixing with the yeasty smell of baking bread. Our bodies
twine, and the big black dog pushes his great head between;
his tail, a metronome, 3/4 time. We'll never get there,
Time is always ahead of us, running down the beach, urging
us on faster, faster, but sometimes we take off our watches,
sometimes we lie in the hammock, caught between the mesh
of rope and the net of stars, suspended, tangled up
in love, running out of time.

A Woman Is Pegging Wash on the Line

She is hanging sheets on rows of rope,
hitching them down with wooden pegs.
She might be pinning clouds to the sky.
They billow and snap like spinnakers.
She is bending over the willow basket,
pegging up sock sock undershirt
        sock sock boxers
        sock sock bra.
She knows the use of the singing line
sure as any fly fisher.
A family of underwear soaks in the sunshine,
bleaches and whitens, like the Day of Redemption.
On the outer circle, the dark and the heavy,
denims and flannels, arms and legs free
to dance a reel and a jig to the fiddling wind.
When the breeze dies down and shadows lengthen,
she reels them in, pulling and tugging.
Squares the corners.
As she hefts the basket, she smells the sun's hot breath,
fresh cut grass, lavender and thyme. She sees the evening
star rise over her roof, and she brings her cargo in.

The Fifties

We spent those stifling endless summer afternoons
on hot front porches, cutting paper dolls from Sears
catalogs, making up our own ideal families
complete with large appliances
and an all-occasion wardrobe with fold-down
paper tabs. Sometimes we left crayons
on the cement landing, just to watch them melt.
We followed the shade around the house.
Time was a jarful of pennies, too hot
to spend, stretching long and sticky,
a brick of Bonomo's Turkish Taffy.
Tomorrow'd be more of the same,
ending with softball or kickball,
then hide and seek in the mosquitoey dark.
Fireflies, like connect-the-dots or find-the-hidden-
words, rose and glowed, winked on and off,
their cool fires coded signals
of longing and love
that we would one day
learn to speak.

Junior High, Home Economics

My best friend and I were in love
with sewing, our old Singers, black as licorice,
gold scrolls and flowers, the name, lettered in Gothic.
The hum, the glide, as miles and miles of seams
ran through the presser foot, straight
as train tracks. The fine mercerized cotton thread,
that wound from spool to bobbin, an intricate dance,
through the tension, around the dial, the take-up
lever, then entered the needle's eye.
The possibilities of an uncut bolt of fabric,
what it might become. Butterick, McCall's, Simplicity,
the rustle of patterns. We dreamed about cloth:
puckery seersuckers, watered silks, crushed velvets,
pinwale and widewale corduroys, dotted Swiss.
Laying out the pattern, a flimsy jigsaw puzzle,
the thin tissue. Finding the straight of the grain,
parallel to the selvage edge. The fat tomato pincushion,
the strawberry needle sharpener. Cut on the bias last.
The slick, the slide of oiled shears. Some seams
have to be eased. Stay stitching, basting, top-
stitching, gathering. Press all seams open, wrong
side of fabric. Cut on curves, clip on notches.
The endless variety of closures: hooks & eyes,
buttons & holes, snaps. I set in her zippers,
she put up my hems; every other day,
we traded clothes in the girls' room
before the last bell. Box pleats, knife pleats,
pin tucks. All those notions: rickrack, twill tape,
corded piping. Plaids, both even and uneven.
My first project, a heather blue and charcoal gray
circle skirt, the fabric wasn't wide enough;
I had to piece an inset to match the plaids.
Even her grandmother looked hard to find the seam.

We didn't know what was coming: the broken marriages,
the sweet babies who turned into teenagers;
couldn't imagine a future that didn't fit
the pattern, thought there was nothing
we couldn't alter, darn, or patch,
somehow make right.

Nearing Menopause, I Run Into Elvis at Shoprite,

near the peanut butter. He calls me ma'am, like the sweet
southern mother's boy he was. This is the young Elvis,
slim-hipped, dressed in leather, black hair swirled
like a duck's backside. I'm in the middle of my life,
the start of the body's cruel betrayals, the skin beginning
to break in lines and creases, the thickening midline.
I feel my temperature rising, as a hot flash washes over,
the thermostat broken down. The first time I heard Elvis
on the radio, I was poised between girlhood and what comes next.
My parents were appalled, in the Eisenhower fifties, by rock
and roll and all it stood for, let me only buy one record,
"Love Me Tender," and I did.
> I have on a tight orlon sweater, circle skirt,
> eight layers of rolled-up net petticoats, all bound
> together by a woven straw cinch belt. Now I've come
> full circle, hate the music my daughter loves, Nine
> Inch Nails, Smashing Pumpkins, Crash Test Dummies.
> Elvis looks embarrassed for me. His soft full lips
> are like moon pies, his eyelids half-mast, pulled
> down bedroom shades. He mumbles, "Treat me nice."
Now, poised between menopause and what comes next, the last
dance, I find myself in tears by the toilet paper rolls,
hearing "Unchained Melody" on the sound system. "That's all
right now, Mama," Elvis says, "Anyway you do is fine." The bass
line thumps and grinds, the honky tonk piano moves
like an ivory river, full of swampy delta blues. And Elvis's voice
wails above it all, the purr and growl, the snarl and twang,
above the chains of flesh and time.

Against Nostalgia

"We're not interested in poems about somebody's dead grandmother.
We want to be elevated, not depressed. Where did the idea come from
that poetry and nostalgia go hand in hand?" —*editorial guidelines*

We don't care how good her eggplant parmagiana was,
or how many afghans she knitted. We don't want to hear
about how your marriage unraveled, an inch at a time,
or your best friend's one on one with the Big C.
Nor do we care where you spent your vacation,
how your luggage got lost on the way to Provence,
or what baggage from childhood you still carry
with you. Nobody wants to read about the schoolroom
where you diagrammed sentences on the blackboard,
then got to clean erasers, clapping up clouds of chalkdust
as a reward. We hate the yellow glow of nostalgia
that seeps out of the windows in the house where you grew up;
we detest the chintz prints, the antimacassars. And we don't
want to hear your scratchy 45s, those golden oldies,
or page through your yearbook, row after row of girls
with bubble cuts and Peter Pan collars. We want to be exalted,
uplifted; we want to soar like red-tailed hawks
on warm thermals, rise above the blood, the dirt, the earth.

VI

The Woman Who Called Hawks from the Sky

All summer long, I hear him, his faint call of blood,
though he stays high up, a speck, a mote, a floater.
His hunger sharpens, honed on the strop of the wind.

In October, he floats on the thermals,
halfway between the flamboyant sky
and the gaudy dance of sugar maple, oak leaf, birch.

When the apples ripen, heavy and red, when gravity
begins to call them down, I hear him high above the clouds
crying, "Killer, killer, killer."

In winter, when water in the birdbath turns to stone,
he comes down in a rush of mottled feathers flame stitched
brown and white, all hooks and curves, talons, beak.

I come to the back door, with my bowl of blood,
chicken scraps, congealed fat, gristle, skin,
leave it as an offering.

When nothing in my life seems predictable or constant,
down he comes, a whistle on the wind, conjured
out of nothing, the great grey ceiling, the thin, thin air.

Van Gogh's Crows

My son has been pacing, wringing his fingers,
flicking from news to weather channels,
as a hurricane moves up the coast.
His panic is palpable, lurks in the murky air
pushed up from the tropics ahead of the storm.
Nothing we say can calm him, as he wears a groove in the rug.
I think of Van Gogh, those wheat fields under the pulsing
sun, the scornful voices of the crows, the writhing blue sky.
Think how hard the simplest action must be
when those voices won't leave you alone,
when even the stars at night throb and gyrate.
My son says his skin crawls, his back is always itchy.
What would it be like to lift from this earth,
rise above a sea of molten gold, scratch
your name on the blue air, "caw caw caw,"
be nothing more than a black pulse beating,
rowing, your way back to God?

Why Monday Mornings Do Not Resemble the Shozui Temple

> where Basho wrote: *A monk sips morning tea,*
> *it's quiet,*
> *the chrysanthemum's flowering.*

Here, the kettle boils over, the microwave chirps
impatiently over the computer's whir, and morning
cartoons murmur mindlessly.

Then the yellow bus comes, with its fanfare of brakes,
and my son races out, slamming the door, which stirs
the dreaming dog into action, a perfunctory chase
of the fat white cat,

whose body resembles the line of clouds floating here
in a long parade over a theatrical backdrop of blue scrim,
watered silk. Now, the rare white tiger of Siberia crouches
in repose, and see, sailing up over the tulip trees,
it's the entire state of Virginia, Roanoke to the Blue Ridge,
the Tidewaters, the Northern suburbs.

From far, far away, Monday is mewling in the corner,
something about the vacuuming,
something about the wash.

But this brilliant scroll keeps unwinding,
and how can I turn away? Look, in the corner,
the calligrapher of trees is inscribing
poem after poem in all the languages of the Orient
that I do not speak, and I must translate them quickly,
one after the other, before the ink dissolves
and the light fails in the west.

Nature Morte au Plat et Pommes
still life by Cézanne (literally, "Dead Nature")

These apples fill the silver bowl
with their roundness, plump globes
of red, yellow, green; you can feel them
fit in the palm of your hand, even though
they're *huile sur toile*, oil on canvas,
imagination, pigment, and air. But
think about apples themselves, all that juice
and sweet flesh, springing from black seeds,
rain and dirt, the first transubstantiation, stemming
from Eden. Who *was* the first gardener, the one
before Adam, who planted winesap pips
and waited, then pruned suckers and water shoots,
thinned the blossoms, defruited and deadheaded,
hoping for a good harvest? No wonder Eve was bedazzled;
they shone like jewels on a velvet tray. The rosy skin,
the satisfying crunch, each succulent bite. And then she cut
slices, fed them to her lover, wedge by dripping wedge,
licked the sugar from his fingers. It wasn't the knowledge
of good and evil after all that opened their eyes, but the hunger
of the body that argues against still life, that says, "I am alive
on this green earth, and I want *more*."

The Unfinished Work in Blue and Gold

will never be completed; no matter how hard I try
to dress it up, shine its shoes, it can only
approximate, never measure up
to what's outside the window calling
"over here over here"

The sky, blue as the robes of Titian's Madonna,
this gold, the leaves of the Osage Orange,
it could come from Monet's haystacks,
but that's not quite right either—

Maybe the gold is a solo by Charlie Parker,
notes turned liquid in the autumn sun,
maybe the blue is the implacable sky
where Van Gogh's church at Auvers
floats off the earth.
On the tape at the Musée d'Orsay,
he said, "I look for the blue."
But you don't have to look hard,
Vincent, my man, the blues
will find you anyway,
even on a starry night.

I sail off in the blue canoe of the sky,
let the sun turn every little hair on my arms gold,
dip my paddle in the water, try again.

October Lights

the woods, and the leaves begin their slow burn,
flame against the sky's hard blue enamel.
This is the long death of the leafy year;
the year my friend's cancer
burned her down to ash and bone.
I'm driving home through the Blue Ridge,
every turn in the road better than the last.
I slip Bonnie Raitt in the cassette deck,
her whisky-fogged voice singing "We got nothin' but time,"
knowing we don't. Soon it will be the Day
of the Dead, when we remember those who've gone
over the shining path, who have left this body
and its basket of pain. These leaves, uncountable
as the stars, could be made of polished metal,
copper or brass, make music when the wind blows through them.
And the sky sings its own long note, a radiant heartache blue.

This Time of Year,

when the light leaves early, sun slipping down
behind the beech trees as easily as a spoon
of cherry cough syrup, four deer step delicately
up our path, just at the moment when the colors
shift, to eat fallen apples in the tall grass.
Great grey ghosts. If we steal outside in the dark,
we can hear them chew. A sudden movement,
they're gone, the whiteness of their tails
a burning afterimage. A hollow pumpkin moon rises,
turns the dried corn to chiaroscuro, shape and shadow;
the breath of the wind draws the leaves and stalks
like melancholy cellos. These days are songs, noon air
that flows like warm honey, the maple trees' glissando
of fat buttery leaves. The sun goes straight to the gut
like a slug of brandy, an eau-de-vie. Ochre October:
the sky, a blue dazzle, the grand finale of trees,
this spontaneous applause; when darkness falls
like a curtain, the last act, the passage of time,
that blue current; October, and the light leaves early,
our radiant hungers, all these golden losses.

Praise Song

Praise the light of late November,
the thin sunlight that goes deep in the bones.
Praise the crows chattering in the oak trees;
though they are clothed in night, they do not
despair. Praise what little there's left:
the small boats of milkweed pods, husks, hulls,
shells, the architecture of trees. Praise the meadow
of dried weeds: yarrow, goldenrod, chicory,
the remains of summer. Praise the blue sky
that hasn't cracked yet. Praise the sun slipping down
behind the beechnuts, praise the quilt of leaves
that covers the grass: Scarlet Oak, Sweet Gum,
Sugar Maple. Though darkness gathers, praise our crazy
fallen world; it's all we have, and it's never enough.

Poem for My Birthday

It's November, light of amber, plum clouded sunsets,
the remaining leaves somber, russets and umber,
the last bits of color before winter's muslin
dropcloths are laid down.

God of the ginkgo trees, whose little lemon fans
have fallen, God of the red oaks, still hanging
on, hear my birthday prayer:

Send me a heart of gratitude for this long afternoon
of goldenrod light falling across my typewriter
and a sky so blue I want to bite it like an apple.

Let me walk in deep leaves on the way to dinner,
scuffling and kicking my Buster Brown shoes
like a nine-year-old girl.

Let the blackboard of the sky be full of stars,
writing all the old stories. When I go back to work,
let me write one good thing that is true.

This afternoon, two crows were arguing off
in the distance; they both want the last word.
So do I.

Poem Ending with a Line by Rumi

White-throated sparrows dart in
and out of the hedgerow,
their sweet long notes rising
above the thicket, the tangle of rosa multiflora,
honeysuckle, and catbriar.
It's late autumn, and everything diminishes.

One winter, a coyote crept down our path, lean and scrawny,
following the ragged thread of his hunger. One year,
a red fox. In the summer of the drought, a black bear.
Our white cat was crouched by the daylilies, thirty feet
away. He flattened himself out like an envelope, shook
for days. The pile of scat remained, full of bird seed
raided from backyard feeders. Each time the dog and I
passed it, I shivered. Something wild came by this way.
Each of these sightings, only once.
A naturalist told me, these small intersections,
our only miracles.

Standing upright, it's hard to see clearly from this height;
we have to get on our hands and knees to find
scarlet pimpernel in the lawn, blue-eyed grass,
or a mourning cloak, the row of cobalt dots hidden
in the black stripes on its tawny wings.

Once, down in the woods, four deer crossed
the road in front of me. It was first frost,
and every blade and twig was etched in white.
Their breath plumes hung in the air long after
they vanished in the underbrush.
The silence was so deep, the only sound, leaf falling on leaf.
There are hundreds of ways to kneel and kiss the ground.

The author of poems published in anthologies and magazines such as *Yankee, The Christian Science Monitor, Smartish Pace, The Beloit Poetry Journal, Nimrod, The Denver Quarterly, The Cream City Review, Poetry International, The Christian Century,* and *America,* Barbara Crooker is the recipient of the 2004 WB Yeats Society of New York Award, the 2004 Pennsylvania Center for the Book Poetry in Public Places Poster Competition, the 2003 Thomas Merton Poetry of the Sacred Award, the 2003 "April Is the Cruelest Month" Award from Poets & Writers, the 2000 *New Millenium Writing's* Y2K competition, the 1997 *Karamu* Poetry Award, and others, including three Pennsylvania Council on the Arts Creative Writing Fellowships, ten residencies at the Virginia Center for the Creative Arts, and a prize from the NEA. A seventeen-time nominee for the Pushcart Prize, she was nominated for the 1997 Grammy Awards for her part in the audio version of the popular anthology, *Grow Old Along With Me—The Best is Yet to Be* (Papier Mache Press). She is the author of ten chapbooks, two of which won prizes in national competitions: *Ordinary Life* won the ByLine Chapbook competition in 2001 and *Impressionism* won the Grayson Books Chapbook competition in 2004. She lives with her husband and son in rural northeastern Pennsylvania; two daughters are grown, and she has one grandson.